MW00949178

CODING FOR BEGINNERS

How To Learn Your Next Programming
Language, Ace Your Programming Interview,
And Land The Coding Job Of Your Dreams

BY-MICHAEL STEVEN

COPYRIGHT © 2020 BY MICHAEL STEVEN
ALL RIGHTS RESERVED.

No part of this book may be reproduced in any form or by any electronic or mechanical means, Including information storage and retrieval systems, without written permission from the author, except for the use of brief quotations in a book review.

TABLE OF CONTENTS

CODE? WHAT'S THIS?

Whether on the web, in the news, or around you, everyone is talking about it: the code is everywhere! In its simplest form, code is a computer language, and the art of using it makes it possible to give instructions to a computer so that it performs a predefined task. The code is a set of numbers and letters that, in a certain order, form a series of instructions for your computer. The code for your computer is the equivalent of DNA for humans.

The evolution of technology that we know automatically also advances the code, which now propels the digital world. Businesses are increasingly dependent on code knowledge in order to stay up to date with technological advances. The code is the basis of the infrastructure behind each website, each smartphone application and each computer program; it even controls the start-up of your microwave! Almost all electrical objects contain some form of code.

Just as humans can understand different languages, computers can understand different code languages like Java, .Net, C ++, Python, R and PHP. Computers operate in binary code (a series of several 1's and 0's), the different code languages translate into binary language. Each program has a different purpose; C, for example, is fairly basic but very useful for creating fairly complex graphics, such as a video game, for example, while a program like JavaScript is mainly used for creating websites. Always check which code language is most appropriate for your purpose.

Learning a new code language is the equivalent of learning a foreign language: it takes practice. Therefore, beyond traditional methods such as evening classes or intensive courses, you can also learn to code in a fun and interactive way. Here are some tips to help you:

Use the applications accessible in an app store

There are a number of mobile applications that can help you learn to code, such as Light-bot (iOS and Android) or Cargo-bot (iOS), which introduce you to the basics. These applications teach you to play by directing a character: you program its movement on a map according to an objective such as transporting pallets from one place to another.

There are many similar apps available on smartphones or tablets - check out your app store to find the one that works best for you.

Applications like Khan Academy offer lessons for learning languages like HTML, JavaScript and C ++. If you have a specific goal in mind, this app can be very useful. The Solo Learn app is also available on all mobile devices (but also on the web) and offers a complete and measured learning experience with nearly 900 lessons available.

On the web, take a look at Codecademy.

Codecademy is a free online tool, perfect for beginners. It offers simple tutorials in most existing code languages. Whether you are interested in Python, Ruby or PHP, or you simply want to try several languages before choosing one, in particular, the platform offers many dot games and other badges that help you learn while having fun.

National Code Learning Week

Wherever you are based, you can be sure that there is a national week of learning code, a great opportunity to learn more and be tempted. In Europe, the CodeWeek which takes place every autumn allows interested people of all levels to participate in workshops and better understand how the code helps in many aspects of everyday life.

Similarly, the United States has its National Coding Week, which presents code and other uses of digital technology to the general public. During this week, schools, businesses and libraries are transformed into learning centers for groups of different levels. These events take place all over the country and represent a good opportunity for beginners to discover different aspects of the code.

Computer Coding, A Term That Means A Lot

Let's start with something simple: when you want to turn on your computer, you don't say, "Hey man, go ahead, wake up, I have to look at something on Google." You press a button, and the computer activates all of its small internal circuits to start.

On the Internet, it's a bit the same thing: a website is not written "in good English" but using computer language.

For example, instead of writing "There you put the title My Perfect Blog," we will write <title>Mon Blog Parfait</title>

Why complicate life like this?

Internet is global - Yes, it's not just the English who create websites, so we had to define rules that everyone could apply, regardless of their country of residence.

The computer is less intelligent than you - Without this "codification" which creates rules common to everyone, the computer would not do. Robert would tell him, "My blog is called My Perfect Blog," Gertrude would tell him, "My blog title is My Perfect Blog" ... Anyway, we would all have different ways of asking for the same thing, and the computer is not still smart enough to understand it.

So we create a "code" that everyone will be able to use, and that does the same thing everywhere. The advantage is also that it allows people around the world to "understand" each other, to help each other. The downside is that well stretched; it can also arouse the lust of hackers who will seek to exploit computer coding errors to take control of a site or destroy it.

In code, we speak several languages

If you go to China, ideally you must speak Chinese... You can get by speaking English in the big cities, but if you want to visit the small provinces, you will have to master Chinese. In IT, it's the same:

There are several languages - Depending on the needs we have, we do not always use the same. Some languages are mainly used to design web pages (like the famous PHP language); others are rather used to create a software (like Java, Perl); others are used, for example, in the world of video games (C #, C ++)...

There are "dominant" languages - In the same way that English is a reference language at the international level, there are in computer science very widely used languages. For example, PHP and Javascript are used by almost all websites.

What about HTML, did you forget about HTML?

In blogging, they0 often talk to you in HTML and CSS tutorials.

What is it about? These are also languages that allow you to give commands to the computer, but they are a bit apart. These are not programming languages but rather languages that allow you to structure a page, organize it, present it. So these are much more basic languages.

For example, "When I started to create websites, we gave all the orders concerning the formatting of a site in HTML. Until the day we realized that it was not very practical.

If I wanted to have my titles in bold and red on all pages, I had to specify it each time, for each title. And obviously, if suddenly I started to want green titles, I had to modify everything by hand, title by title. I said to myself, "Ah, if only we could say once and for all to the site to put ALL the titles in bold and red! And there, someone invented CSS."

CSS allows you to format a website by defining major rules that will apply to several elements of the site or even the entire site. It is, therefore, complementary to HTML.

On the blog, for example, when I want to put a little bit of bold text, I do it in HTML. But when I want my little titles to always appear in mustard yellow with a line below, I do it in CSS to avoid having to repeat each time "this title is yellow, there is a line in-below which is such a thickness, etc."

Remember that HTML is a language to organize the page ... and CSS a language to format it define its design.

Logic in computer code

HTML and CSS just do what they are told to do, but there is no real logic in these languages. The text is in bold or not, period. This is the basis when you want to modify the design of your site.

Then, if we want to go further, we can learn a programming language like PHP. The PHP allows this time to play with the logic of the site.

You can create "scenarios" and define what happens for each scenario. "If we are on the home page, then you will display the title in red. Otherwise, you will display the title in green". On a blog, it allows, for example, to display a different sidebar depending on the section in which we are.

HTML and CSS are a little like sheep; they follow your orders with the finger and the eye. PHP is a leader who will be able to do strategy: if something happens, then we will have to react like that.

Should we learn computer coding?

Today, blogging platforms are rather easy to use, even when you know no computer language.

You are an amateur blogger

If you want to do it without technique, it is possible. Nevertheless, it is very useful for a blogger to know HTML.

It is thanks to this language that you will understand how your blog is organized and structured: why a text becomes bold when you would like it not, why an image is displayed on the right and how to center it, why your social media icons are not aligned properly...

Mastering HTML makes it possible to solve a lot of small problems that we encounter on a daily basis, but above all, it allows us to personalize our blog easily: colors, putting an image or a logo, etc.

There are other advantages:

If you have understood the logic of HTML, you will also easily understand that of CSS because the two languages go together.

Once you have an excellent grasp of HTML and are used to seeing the code on a page, you will be able to switch to other languages more easily. It's just like when you type on a keyboard. At first, your fingers do not know where the keys are located, so you type slowly, and after a while, your fingers strum on their own without you having to think about the position of the keys. In IT, once HTML has become an "automatism," you can more easily focus on the other languages present, such as PHP.

You will also know more easily how to use the ready-made "bits of code" found on the Internet to add this or that functionality to its site.

PHP and other languages, you will often want to get started on it the day you come across a situation where your knowledge is not enough to do what you have in mind.

You blog professionally

If you run a blog with professional ambitions (business blog, blog to promote your skills), it goes without saying that it requires a more thorough approach.

The computer coding is a way to customize its visual identity to create a more effective website, improve ergonomics.

In this situation...

Either you do not want to manage this ... because you do not like the technique: in which case, call a professional to relieve you of this technical part. Yes, it is an investment, but this investment saves you time that you can put at the service of tasks that you better control and that are useful for your activity: create content, improve your offer, pamper your customers...

Either you want to manage this: in this case, train yourself! Today there are a host of MOOCs and online resources to learn how to code. Be aware that it will take time to master everything and that you may need a third party boost, at least at the start!

Computer coding, an ongoing challenge

Most of the time, HTML and CSS are learned "on the job". When you write a blog post, you often write through a "visual editor" that shows you the final rendering of your text and where you just have to click a button to italicize or underline it. But there is also an HTML editor that shows you the same text formatted with HTML. From time to time, have fun switching from one to the other. You will quickly understand the main lines of HTML.

What is programming

In computer science, programming is the realization of a series of tasks divided into five stages: analysis, design, coding, testing, and maintenance.

Today, the computer is an indispensable tool in many fields, such as medicine, astronomy, communications, etc. Thanks to information technology, there have been technological advances that were unthinkable before the so-called "computer revolution." However, the machine can do absolutely nothing without software, that is, without a program that tells you what you have to do. But how is a program made?

Currently, almost all the hardware that exists in the world is manufactured in series, unlike with the software, which is mostly developed as.

Custom software, usually, is usually a computer application developed by a company - software developer - for another company - called a client -, in order to computerize part of the data it manages. Custom software can manage, for example, the sale of airport tickets, the rental of movies from a video store, the medical records of patients in a hospital, etc. In each of these cases, the software needs are different, since they handle different types of information. Even between two airports, two video clubs, or two hospitals, the treatment of the information is usually different. For this reason, the software developed for each of these client companies must be tailored, that is, different from all others.

On the other hand, there is also software that is not tailored, for example, word processors, games, electronic encyclopedias, etc.

Applications of this type are usually aimed at all users of computers (PCs, mobiles, tablets ...) in general and, to a lesser extent, companies.

Programming Methodology

To develop any type of software, a series of techniques and scientific knowledge related to computer science must be put into practice. These techniques and knowledge are grouped into a discipline called programming methodology. However, this discipline is home to different programming paradigms, including structured programming and object-oriented programming.

Although, among these paradigms, many aspects may be similar, others are very different. For example, structured programming is based on three main aspects:

- Application of modular design.
- Use -exclusively- of sequential, alternative, and repetitive structures.
- Use of adequate data structures to manipulate information.
- On the other hand, more advanced techniques are used in object-oriented programming: inheritance, polymorphism, etc.

Software engineering

The production process of any computer application involves carrying out a series of tasks divided into five stages, called: analysis, design, coding, testing, and maintenance. These five phases are known as the life cycle of a software product, or in other words, the life cycle of a program is the different stages through which it has to go through its existence.

Stages of the life cycle of a program.

All the tasks of the software development process must be planned, that is, for each of them, the approximate start date and end date must be established. In addition, all tasks must be controlled throughout the entire production process; that is, continuous monitoring of the computer project must be carried out. This entire process of software production and management is known as Software Engineering.

Software quality

Software Engineering is used primarily to develop large-scale applications - of thousands or millions of instructions - where different teams of people and, sometimes, different software companies usually participate. They are usually projects that can last several months or even years. However, however small a software project may be, it is always convenient to apply the principles of Software Engineering, as this will help to develop higher-quality software. The quality of a program can be measured based on three main aspects:

- Its operational characteristics. It should be assessed if the software does what is expected of it (correction) and if, for this, the resources of the computer (efficiency) are optimally used, such as memory, CPU time, etc. It should also be evaluated if the application offers an appropriate user interface (ease of use) and if it is safe with respect to the data (integrity).

- Your ability to undergo changes. In this sense, it is important to estimate the extent to which the program is likely to be corrected (ease of maintenance) or changed (flexibility). We must also see if it is easy to test its operation (ease of testing).

- Its adaptability to different environments. You have to ask yourself to what extent some of this software could be used again in another project (reusability). Likewise, it should be assessed whether the software can interact with other computer systems (interoperability facility) and if it can be used on another machine that uses a different processor (portability), even if it is making small changes to the software.

All the factors that influence the quality of a software project must be measured throughout its development process, that is, in the course of all stages of the life cycle, and not just at the end. In this way, the quality of the resulting software product can be improved on the fly.

The various phases of the life cycle of a program must be performed sequentially. In each of the stages, documentation will be generated that will serve to start the next one. This process is known as a classic or cascade life cycle and is the fundamental basis on which Software Engineering relies.

There are other types or models of life cycles, such as classic with prototype, automatic, spiral, etc. But, all of them are based in some way on the classic model.

Program Encoding

Once the algorithms of an application have been designed, the coding phase can begin. At this stage, these algorithms have to be translated into a specific programming language, in our case C; that is, the actions defined in the algorithms we will convert into instructions, also called sentences, of the C language.

EXAMPLE when coding in C, the algorithm of the program Add, seen in the previous section (Design), something similar to:

```c
#include <stdio.h>

int main()
{
    int a, b, c;

    printf( "\n   Introduzca el primer n%cmero (entero): ", 163 );

    scanf( "%d", &a );

    printf( "\n   Introduzca el segundo n%cmero (entero): ", 163 );

    scanf( "%d", &b );

    c = a + b;

    printf( "\n   La suma es: %d", c );


    return 0;

}
```

To encode an algorithm, you have to know the syntax of the language to which it will be translated. However, regardless of the programming language in which a program is written, it will be its algorithm that determines its logic. The logic of a program establishes what its actions are and in what order they should be executed. Therefore, it is convenient for every programmer to learn to design algorithms before moving on to the coding phase.

Programming languages

A programming language can be defined as an artificial language that allows you to write the instructions of a computer program, or put another way; a programming language allows the programmer to communicate with the computer to tell him what he has to do. To this end, man has invented many programming languages, but all of them can be classified into three main types: the machine, low level, and high level.

The machine language is the only one who understands the digital computer, which is their "natural language." Only two symbols can be used on it: zero (0) and one (1). Therefore, machine language is also called binary language. The computer can only work with bits; however, it is not easy for the programmer to write instructions such as:

10100010

11110011

00100010

00010010

For this reason, more understandable programming languages were invented for the programmer. Thus, low-level languages appeared, also called assembly languages, which allow the programmer to write the instructions of a program using abbreviations, also called mnemonic words, such as ADD, DIV, SUB, etc., instead of use zeros and ones. For example, the instruction:

ADD a, b, c

It could be the translation of the action:

$c \leftarrow a + b$

This action is present in the Add algorithm of the previous section (Design), which indicated that in the memory space represented by the variable c, the sum of the two numbers stored in the memory spaces represented by the variables a and b.

A program written in an assembly language has the disadvantage that it is not understandable to the computer since it is not composed of zeros and ones. To translate the instructions of a program written in an assembly language to instructions of a machine language, you must use a program called an assembler

An added difficulty to binary languages is the fact that they are dependent on the machine - or rather, the processor - that is, each processor uses a different machine language - a different set of instructions - that is defined in its own hardware. Consequently, a program written for a type of processor cannot be used on other equipment that uses a different processor, since the program will not be portable or portable. For this program to work on a second computer, all the instructions written in the machine language of the first computer must be translated into the binary language of the second computer, which is a very expensive and complex job for the programmer.

Likewise, since the instructions that can be written in an assembly language are always associated with the binary instructions of a particular computer, assembly languages are also processor dependent. However, high-level languages are independent of the processor, that is, a program written on any computer with high-level language can be transported to any other computer, with small changes or even none.

A high-level language allows the programmer to write the instructions of a program using words or syntactic expressions very similar to English. For example, in C, you can use words such as case, if, for, while, etc. to build with the instructions like:

if (numero > 0) print("El n%cmero es positivo", 163);

if the number is greater than zero, then write the message on the screen: "The number is positive."

This is the reason why these languages are considered high level because words of very easy compression can be used for the programmer. In contrast, low-level languages are those that are closer to the "understanding" of the machine. Other high-level languages are Ada, BASIC, COBOL, FORTRAN, Pascal, etc.

Another important feature of high-level languages is that, for most of the instructions in these languages, several instructions in an assembly language would be needed to indicate the same. In the same way that, most of the instructions of an assembly language, also groups several instructions of a machine language.

On the other hand, a program written in a high-level language also does not get rid of the inconvenience of the fact that it is not understandable to the computer and, therefore, to translate the instructions of a program written in a high-level language to instructions of a machine language, you have to use another program that, in this case, is called a compiler.

Compilers and interpreters

The instruction set written in a high-level language is called the source code of the program. Thus, the compiler is a program that receives as input data the source code of a program written by a programmer and generates as output a set of instructions written in the binary language of the computer where they will be executed. The set of instructions generated by the compiler is called the object code of the program, also known as machine code or binary code, since it is, in itself, a program executable by the machine.

Normally, a C programmer will use an editing program to write the source code of a program and save it in a file with the extension (.c). For example, "Add.c". Next, a C compiler will translate the source code into object code, saving it with another extension, which, depending on the operating system, may vary. For example, in Windows, it will be saved with the extension (.obj), short for an object.

On the other hand, there is a type of program called interpreter, which also serves to translate the source code of a program into object code, but its way of acting is different from that of a compiler.

The operation of an interpreter is characterized by translating and executing, one by one, the instructions of the source code of a program, but without generating as output object code. The process performed by an interpreter is as follows: read the first instruction of the source code, translate it into object code and execute it; then do the same with the second instruction; and so on, until you reach the last instruction of the program, as long as there is no error that stops the process. In a program, there can be basically three types of errors: syntax, execution, and logic.

Types Of Errors

When a syntax error exists in any instruction of the source code of a program, this error will prevent both the compiler and the interpreter from translating said instruction, since neither of them will understand what the programmer is saying. For example, if instead of the instruction:

print("\n   Introduzca el primer n%cmero (entero): ", 163);

A programmer writes:

prrintf("\n   Introduzca el primer n%cmero (entero): ", 163);

When the compiler or the interpreter reads this line of code, neither of them will understand what prrintf is and, therefore, they will not know how to translate this instruction into machine code; therefore, both will stop the translation and notify the programmer with a message of error.

In summary, syntax errors are detected in the process of translating the source code into binary code. On the contrary that it happens with the errors of execution and of logic that can only be detected when the program is running.

A runtime error occurs when the computer cannot execute any instructions correctly. For example, the instruction:

c = 5 / 0;

It is syntactically correct and will be translated into binary code. However, when the computer tries to perform the division:

5 / 0

An execution error will occur since, mathematically; it cannot be divided by zero.

As for logic errors, they are the most difficult to detect. When a program has no syntax or execution errors but still does not work well, this is due to the existence of some logical error. So, a logic error occurs when the results obtained are not as expected. For example, if instead of the instruction:

c = a + b;

A programmer would have written:

c = a * b;

Until the result of the operation was shown on the screen, the programmer could not realize the error, provided he already knew the result of the sum in advance. In this case, the programmer could easily notice the error, but when the operations are more complex, the logic errors can be very difficult to detect.

Phases of setting up a program

In addition to everything seen so far, we must also take into account that a computer application is usually composed of a set of programs or subprograms. Therefore, the object code of all of them must be linked (linked) to obtain the desired executable program. For this, a program called linker is used, which will generate and save, on disk, an executable file. In Windows, this file will have an extension (.exe), short for executable.

Because high-level languages are portable, a program written in this type of language can be run on any other machine. But, this is not true, since, for this to be possible between machines of different types; the source code of said program must be compiled and linked back to that other machine. This means that, in reality, source codes are portable - even with minor changes - but not binary codes.

For most programs written in high-level programming languages, the process of obtaining the executable code consists of three phases: editing, compilation, and linking. However, some languages and C is a pioneer in this regard, require another phase, called preprocessing. In this stage, a program called preprocessor participates. Preprocessing is always done before compilation; in fact, it is the compiler itself who calls the preprocessor before translating the source code into object code.

The preprocessor serves to make a series of modifications to the source code written by the programmer. Such modifications serve, among other things, so that the linker can later join the object code of the program being developed with the object code of other programs.

Actually, the preprocessing is not visible to the programmer, since the preprocessor does not save any files to disk; it simply modifies the source code and passes it to the compiler so that it can be translated.

Finally, for the executable code of a program to run on the computer, it is necessary that another program in the operating system, called a loader, takes it to its main memory. From that moment on, the CPU will start running it.

Integrated Development Environments (EID)

In the market, there are computer applications, called Integrated Development Environments (EID), which include all the programs necessary to carry out all the phases of setting up a program; in the case of C, you need an editor, a preprocessor, a compiler, and a linker. In addition, an EID usually provides other very useful software tools for programmers, such as code debuggers, online language help, etc. All this, in order to help and facilitate the work of the programmer.

Code debuggers

A code debugger allows the programmer to execute a program step by step, that is, instruction by instruction, stopping the execution in each one of them, and displaying on-screen what is happening in the computer memory at each moment, that is, what values are taking the program variables. In this way, the programmer can check if the program execution thread is the desired one. Otherwise, this may be due to various causes. The first thing to do is check if the algorithm has been translated correctly, since, the programmer may have missed some instruction, or he may have put a plus sign (+) where a minus sign should go (-), etc. In these cases, correcting the error will only affect the source code of the program. However, if the translation of the algorithm is correct, then the problem will be precisely in the design of said algorithm, which will have to be reviewed, modified, and re-encoded.

Testing of a program

Once the executable code of a debugged program is obtained as much as possible, its functionality must be thoroughly checked. To do this, it must be executed as many times as necessary, providing different input data each time and checking whether the output data is always as expected.

The executable code of a program is impossible to have syntax errors since these will have been detected by the compiler and corrected by the programmer. Therefore, the tests to be carried out should focus on the search for execution or logic errors.

To be totally sure of the proper functioning of a program, you should try all possible input combinations, which is usually impossible, since these could be infinite. Thus, the tests have to be very well chosen, trying to cover as many cases as possible, and testing the program in critical aspects.

EXAMPLE The executable code of the program Sum of the previous section (Coding) can be tested with different random input data, such as 3 and 5, 10 and 20, 400 and 56, etc. —All of them positive— knowing in advance that the output data should be: 8, 30 and 456, respectively. It should also be tested if it works correctly with negative numbers, for example, with the numbers: -3 and -5, -10 and -20, etc. Another test that can be done is to add positive numbers with negatives: -3 and 5, 72 and -72, etc. If all the tests have gone well, then you can think that the program works correctly, although you will never be 100% sure, since all cases have not been tested.

In addition, unexpected situations may occur in all programs, that is, situations not provided by the programmer. In those cases, the program will react unpredictably. For example: what will happen if the user enters two letters instead of two whole numbers? What if he enters two real numbers? What will happen if two whole numbers of ten digits each are entered? What if they are thirty figures each? etc.

In a program as simple as Sumar's, the tests to be carried out may take a short time. However, when a large application is developed, the tests may take weeks or even months. Think, for example, of the application that controls the air traffic of an airport, in which it manages all the traffic lights of a large city or in which it supervises the launch of a rocket, etc. In all these examples, the tests should not only focus on the verification of the data processing, but also on aspects such as the adaptation of the application to the rest of the computer system or the interaction of the software with other existing applications. A computer application of such size can be made up of hundreds or thousands of programs, and all of them must be tested individually and together. Before implementing software with these characteristics,

To correct the execution or logic errors found in the testing phase, almost always, if not always, the algorithm must be modified and, in some cases, the problem must even be re-analyzed, going through all the development phases; from which it follows that the better the analysis and design of an application, the probability of finding errors in the testing phase will be lower.

Analysis of a program

Software is always created to solve the problem. Now, not all the problems posed by humans can be computerized. To determine if this is possible, the first thing to do is analyze the problem in question. This involves determining what the demands of the problem are and studying whether it can be solved by putting into practices the techniques and scientific knowledge that can be used in Software Engineering. In the event that it is considered viable, a very thorough analysis of the problem must be carried out, the result of which documentation will be obtained, which will clearly specify which are the requirements that the program must have, understanding these as characteristics that the program will own. This document is called a specification of Software Requirements (ERS), and it will be written what the program to be developed has to do, both in terms of internal behavior (data management) and external (interaction with the user and others Applications).

Software Requirements Specification (ERS)

The ERS is a contract between the developer and the client company. Both parties must communicate very closely to establish the requirements of the application. A good ERS will help the client company describe what it wants, and it will also help developers understand what exactly they are asking for. The final result of the software product depends on the ERS. Therefore, it is very important that it describes in more detail "everything" that is expected of such software. You have to know everything; you even have to know why you don't know what you don't know. To do this, the developer must ask the client questions such as:

- What should the program do? This is the most important question; from it, all the others will arise. The client must explain to the developer what he needs software for, what tasks he wants to perform, in what field, etc.

- What input and output data are involved in the process? All programs manipulate data. Therefore, this is the second most important question, from which others are also derived, such as: is it necessary to validate or filter the input data? How much information is it? Is it always the same? Store the output data in some computer support? Etc.

- What machine and the operating system will it run on? When developing a large application, special attention must be paid to the resources necessary for its proper functioning. In relation to this aspect, some other questions are: is it going to run on a network? Is the speed of the process a critical aspect?

- Who will be the user of the application? It is not the same to develop an application to be used by people who have advanced computer skills (for example, a network administrator) than by others who only have user-level knowledge (for example, an administrator). This aspect will influence, in particular, how the application interface should be, and what are the terms in which the user manual will be prepared. The user manual of any program is usually a book that accompanies the software. This manual can be prepared throughout the life cycle, and it explains to the user the steps to follow to install the application, configure it, use it, etc. Sometimes, computer applications also offer online help, which is also part of that documentation.

In addition, it is necessary to know other things, such as: What will be the treatment of possible errors in the execution of the program? How will the security of the data be guaranteed?, what will be the useful life of the application?, Can it undergo modifications in the future? Etc.

When you intend to develop a very large application, your ERS can be very extensive, of several tens or hundreds of pages. On the contrary, the ERS of the problem in the following example can be written in a few lines, because the program to be developed is very small; but, at the same time, it is very illustrative.

EXAMPLE Suppose that someone who has hardly any computer skills asks a friend, "computer programmer," to make a program that can be used to add any two whole numbers. The conversation between the two protagonists could be the following:

"What program do you need?"

"I need a program to do sums."

"What kind of sums?"

"Of two whole numbers."

"Are you going to enter them by keyboard?"

-Yes.

—Will the result be displayed on the screen?

-Yes.

"What computer are you going to run it on?"

-In mine.

- What characteristics does it have?

—Sixteen gigabytes of RAM, 500 gigabytes of the hard drive ...

- Super and operating system?

—Windows 10.

"Well, I think I have everything."

From the conversation between the two friends, you can obtain an ERS where you must specify that the program must perform the following tasks:

- First, the program must ask for two numbers by keypad (integer data).
- Next, it will calculate the sum of the two numbers entered by the user.
- Finally, you have to show the result obtained on the screen (whole data).

The screen will show, for example:

On-screen display of a program that performs the sum of two integers.

Thus, it has been described what is expected to do the program Add, that is, its functionality has been explained.

On the other hand, the ERS would also have to specify who will be the user of the program and on which computer and operating system it will be executed. On this occasion, the user does not require advanced computer skills, since it will not even be necessary to develop a software user manual. As for the operating system and performance of the machine, since it is such a simple program, in principle, any computer in the current market will serve.

When an application works with a large volume of information, it is normal for the ERS to also include a detailed description of the data to be manipulated. In this case, it is enough to say that in the process; only three data will be involved: two whole numbers of entry and one of output.

Design of a program

Once the requirements of a program have been established, the design phase can begin. At this stage, you have to find a computer solution to the problem posed. This solution will determine how the problem will be solved.

As a general rule, it is usually not easy to find an optimal solution and, even less, when the problem has a certain size. To find such a solution, the developer can make use of the modular design.

Modular design

Given a problem to be solved, we must first study whether there is the possibility of dividing it into smaller ones, called subproblems (this method is known as "divide and conquer"). Each of them can be treated in isolation; therefore, the overall complexity of the problem will decrease considerably. Similarly, if the subproblems obtained remain too complicated, it may also be convenient to fragment them. And so on, until you reach really simple subproblems.

EXAMPLE Assuming that you want to develop an application to manage the rental of movies from a video store and that your ERS details the way in which said the software will treat the data of the partners (name, surname, address, etc.), of the films (title, director, duration, etc.) and rentals (loan date, return date, etc.), in this case, the main problem can be broken down into three smaller ones: partner management, management movies, and rental management. Each of which can also be fragmented. For example, movie management could be broken down into high, low, modifications, and queries. And so on, as long as it is considered appropriate.

Each subproblem is considered part or module of the global problem, and each of them will be solved through a program or subprogram.

Depending on the characteristics of each problem and derived subproblems, a different level of decomposition will be achieved. To the person who performs the analysis, these characteristics will serve to abstract as much as possible the problem and subproblems to solve. The abstraction allows each subproblem considered separately, in isolation from others.

The modules interrelate with each other since each of them will have a behavior that will affect the one above or below it. However, the way in which each module performs its tasks will not be visible to the rest of the modules; this is known as encapsulation.

In summary, the solution to a problem is usually given by a program represented by the main module, which is broken down into subprograms (submodules), which, in turn, can also be divided, and so on, that is, the problem is solved from top to bottom. This method is called a modular or top-down design.

What Is An Algorithm?

In the coding phase, all the modules defined by the modular design will become a program; that is, the final application will consist of the sum of all the programs that are designed. But first, we must determine what the instructions or actions of each of these programs are. To do this, algorithms must be used.

An algorithm establishes, in a generic and informal way, the sequence of steps or actions that solves a certain problem. The algorithms constitute the main documentation that is needed to be able to start the coding phase, and, to represent them, two types of notation are essentially used: pseudocode and flowcharts. The design of an algorithm is independent of the language that will later be used to encode it.

Pseudocode

The pseudocode is an algorithmic programming language; It is an intermediate language between natural language and any specific programming language, such as C, FORTRAN, Pascal, etc. There is no formal or standard pseudocode notation, but each programmer can use their own. Now, in the example algorithms in this tutorial and others in Abrirllave,

EXAMPLE Given the specifications of the example in the previous section (Analysis) for a program that will calculate the sum of any two whole numbers entered by the user and then display the result obtained on the screen, since it is a problem very simple, in this case, it is not essential to break it down into smaller ones. Consequently, the resulting program will consist of a single module. The algorithm of this module, written in pseudocode CEE, can be the following:

algoritmo Sumar

variables

  entero a, b, c

inicio

  escribir("Introduzca el primer número (entero): ")

  leer(a)

  escribir("Introduzca el segundo número (entero): ")

  leer(b)

  $c \leftarrow a + b$

  escribir("La suma es: ", c)

fin

An algorithm written in pseudocode is usually organized in three sections: header, declarations, and body. In the header section, the name of the algorithm is written, in this case, add. In the declarations section, some of the objects that the program will use are declared. In the tutorial of the language of Abrirllave, the different types of objects that can be used in a program are studied in detail, such as variables, constants, subprograms, etc. For now, note that, in this example, the variables a, b, and c, they indicate that the program needs three spaces in the main memory of the computer to store three integers. Each of the variables refers to a different memory space.

In the body, all the actions that have to be carried out in the program are described, and they are always written between the words start and end. The first action:

write ("Enter the first number (integer):")

Indicates that the message in double quotes should be displayed on the screen. Then, through the action:

leer(a)

It is being indicated that the program will wait for the user to type an integer, which will be stored in the memory space represented by the variable a. The same process must be followed with the second number, which will be stored in the memory space represented by the variable b.

write ("Enter the second number (integer):")leer(b)

Then the action:

$c \leftarrow a + b$

It indicates that the sum of the two numbers entered by the program user must be stored in the memory space represented by the variable c. Finally, the result of the sum will be displayed on the screen with the action:

write ("The sum is:", c)

Flowcharts (Ordinograms)

Algorithms can also be represented, graphically, by means of flowcharts. Flowcharts can be used for other purposes; however, in this tutorial, we will only use them to represent algorithms. Such flow charts are also known as audiograms. In other words, an ordinogram graphically represents the order of the steps or actions of an algorithm.

Pseudocode and flowcharts are the two most used tools to design algorithms in structured programming. Although, between both types of representation, there are the following important differences:

Flowcharts began to be used before the pseudocode.

In pseudocode, three sections of the algorithm are usually defined (header, declarations, and body). However, in one ordinogram only the body is represented.

In an ordinogram it is usually easier to see, at first glance, what the order of the algorithm's actions is.

The graphic symbols used in a flowchart have been standardized by the American National Standards Institute (ANSI). However, there is no "standard pseudocode."

Qualities of an algorithm

For any given problem there is no single algorithmic solution; It is the task of the person who designs an algorithm to find the most optimal solution, this is none other than one that more faithfully meets the desirable qualities of any well-designed algorithm:

- Finitude. An algorithm always has to end after a finite number of actions. When the Add algorithm is already a program, its execution will always be the same, since, the actions described in the body of the algorithm will always be followed, one by one, from the first to the last and in the established order.

- Accuracy. All the actions of an algorithm must be well defined, that is, no action can be ambiguous, but each one of them must only be interpreted in a unique way. In other words, if the program resulting from an algorithm is executed several times with the same input data, in all cases, the same output data will be obtained.

- Clarity. Normally, a problem can be solved in different ways. Therefore, one of the most important tasks of the designer of an algorithm is to find the most readable solution, that is, the most understandable for the human being.

- Generality. An algorithm must solve general problems. For example, the Add program should be used to make sums of any two whole numbers, and not only to add two specific numbers, such as 3 and 5.

- Efficiency. The execution of the program resulting from coding an algorithm should consume as little as possible the available resources of the computer (memory, CPU time, etc.).

- Simplicity. Sometimes, finding the most efficient algorithmic solution to a problem can lead to writing a very complex algorithm, affecting its clarity. Therefore, we must try to make the solution simple, even at the cost of losing a bit of efficiency, that is, we must find a balance between clarity and efficiency. Writing simple, clear, and efficient algorithms is achieved based on practice.

- Modularity. Never forget the fact that an algorithm can be part of the solution to a bigger problem. But, in turn, this algorithm must be broken down into others, as long as this favors its clarity.

The person who designs an algorithm must be aware that all the properties of an algorithm will be transmitted to the resulting program.

Maintenance of a program

The maintenance of the software can be done basically in two ways: repair or modification. Once the application is implemented, errors not detected in the previous phases can still occur, which will involve making repairs. On the other hand, it may be that the application wants to expand or change some functionality, which will lead to modifications.

EXAMPLE

The Add program might be required to also add two real numbers. To make this modification, the program must change its ERS, revise its algorithm, rewrite its source code, obtain the new executable file, and perform new tests.

In a small program, modifications or repairs can be easy to make. However, in large applications, a small modification or repair can be very expensive. In addition, we must have in mind that although the software can never be damaged, as it can happen to the hardware, the software can deteriorate due to the changes. So much so that, in some cases, it may be preferable to start the entire application from scratch, so the old software can stop being used when it becomes obsolete, which means the end of its existence, that is, the end of its cycle of life. This has always happened, for example, with some older operating systems, with management applications that have been discontinued due to the appearance of much more functional ones,

Program Documentation

In order for the maintenance of a computer application to be as easy as possible, it is convenient to have all its documentation, that is, all the documents that have been generated in all the previous stages: ERS, algorithms, source codes, user manuals, etc. All this type of documentation is considered external. In addition, there is another type of documentation called internal.

The internal documentation of a program is the comments that the programmer can write in the source code of a program and that the compiler will not take into account since they are not instructions. The comments of a program are explanations or clarifications that will help the programmer in the future when he wants to review or modify the source code of the said program, and they will still be more helpful if the modification has to be done by a programmer other than the one who wrote the code source at first.

Coding And Programming. What Is The Difference?

Coding and programming are often used interchangeably in the industry. Both terms may seem the same from the outside, but there is a significant difference between them. Today, we will try to explain the difference between coding and programming in the easiest way possible.

Coding

Coding means writing codes from one language to another. Computers do not understand our language. They only understand binary language. A programmer is someone who translates the requirements into a language that a machine will understand. Although there are many intermediate processes, what an encoder does is translate the logic into machine-readable codes.

The coding is a part of the program or can be considered as the initial step of programming. According to the instruction, the term "programming" is used in a much broader sense. A programmer works on the instructions provided by the team leaders, so coding is easier and requires less experience than programming.

Programming

Programming is the largest image that involves more things than just writing code. It is basically a machine feeding process with a set of instructions to do what you want.

A programmer designs analyze a problem, develops logic, and ensures that a machine or application will run without errors. An encoder writes code at an intermediate level, while a programmer is responsible for finding effective solutions to potential problems that may or may not be related to the process.

A programmer cannot simply sit down and write code to achieve specific functionalities. He or she also deals with the smallest problems that can ruin the code along with all the schedules. The programmers do the planning part and navigate the project accordingly for the successful implementation of the product without errors or errors.

A programmer can work as a programmer, developer, analyst, etc. and, therefore, it takes more years to become an experienced professional programmer.

Coding is writing a chapter; programming is creating a book

If you are still confused between coding and programming, let me explain it with some simple examples. Suppose Chinse is a programming language. Now, an encoder is a person who knows English at the basic level and can write a short story on it.

On the other hand, a programmer is a person who knows English quite well and can produce long articles or other long jobs with ease.

Python

it is the most commonly taught language in school and is also at the forefront of advanced technologies, including artificial intelligence and machine learning. This imply that there will be a lot of jobs for Python developers in the future, which will make it a good language for learning and mastering the language.

If you like Python sound, there are many resources to help you get started. BitDegree offers two separate Python courses. The first will teach you the basics of Python coding through an engaging video tutorial, while the second will provide you with a practical learning experience that will allow you to train as you learn.

Java

With Python, Java has the most versatile and widely used computer programming languages in the world. It is primarily used for back-end web development and the creation of mobile applications but is by no means limited to them.

Historically, the vast majority of native Android applications have been created using Java. While this is evolving slowly, there will be high demand for developers to look to the future to maintain and update existing applications, as well as to create new applications.

One of the main advantages of Java is its scalability. This has made it one of the languages most used by the largest and most successful websites in the world. It is also relatively easy to use, simple to learn.

If you want to learn Java, you can start with one of BitDegree's online courses. The Java interactive course will teach you the basics of 'What is coding' with a focus on Java. Designed for beginners, you will come out with enough knowledge to really launch your programming career.

JavaScript

The last language on our list, JavaScript (not to be confused with Java), has been one of the fastest-growing languages in recent years. The growing demand for JavaScript developers has resulted in a major shortage, making it a language of choice for many new programmers.

JavaScript has traditionally been used for the development of front-end websites to create interactive displays. It controls elements such as video players, animations, and GIFs. However, recently, JavaScript has been used more and more for back-end development, which means that you can theoretically develop the majority of your website using the same language.

Like the other languages described above, JavaScript is a good choice if you are just starting out with programming. It's relatively simple, and there is a wide range of resources that learners can rely on. An online course, like the interactive JavaScript tutorial, is a good place to start.

How can I speed up my learning?

Now that we have answered the question, "What is computer coding? "It's time to think about learning your mother tongue. It is important to realize that learning a new programming language is not necessarily easy, even if you choose one of the simplest languages like HTML or Python. It will take a lot of time and dedication to learn the syntax and conventions of the language, but to be able to speak fluently; you will need a lot of practice.

In addition to the online courses mentioned throughout the article, there are many resources available to help you learn faster, including:

- Videos. Visit YouTube to watch hundreds of videos with the main features of the language of your choice.
- Textbooks. If you really want to learn computer coding, you should consider getting your hands on two good textbooks that describe things like syntax and other tools.
- Games. With the increase in coding, the number of applications and games designed to teach you how to program has increased. Although many of them are for children, they can still be a great way to practice.

The practice is the most important thing to master a language. How you practice doesn't really matter - as long as you spend time on it, you will improve.

It's time to move on to learning

Computer coding

You may have a vague idea of the different programming languages and the fact that they are used to create websites and applications, but you know a lot more!

If you are interested in computer coding and want to deepen your knowledge, the next step is to choose a language to learn. Try to find the one that interests you that will allow you to work in a field of your choice - the languages described above are just a few of these languages, so be sure to do a lot of research before choosing a language.

The advantages of Python Software

1. Open Source

Python is a completely open-source programming language. This means that it is free to use, and everyone can fully view the code. This allows developers to easily customize Python to meet their specific needs and requirements.

In addition, it ensures that no organization can terminate Python or impose restrictions on further development. It will always be free to use, and an enthusiastic community makes Python one of the most interesting and powerful programming languages you can use for your project.

Since Python is completely open-source, the base code is well known. All future modifications to a project programmed in Python will, therefore, not be too complicated thanks to the user-friendly design. Unlike proprietary software, you're not tied to a slow-developing, limited system that slows down your projects and makes licensing difficult.

2. User-friendly and easy to learn

Python's clear and easy to understand syntax has made it one of the world's most user-friendly programming languages. It is used in many projects worldwide, ranging from small-scale programs for Raspberry PI to huge projects at NASA and Google.

If anyone, from beginner to expert, can understand and use a programming language effectively, that is a good sign.

Anyone who is familiar with Matlab, C / C ++, Visual Basic, or Java will quickly master the basics of Python and will be able to program in Python faster than ever before, because many brackets and semicolons, which sometimes make other programming languages difficult are simply no longer required. This is a major advantage of Python, as it means that beginners can jump in, understand the code relatively easily, and make minor adjustments without messing up the system.

Python has an enthusiastic and fanatic community that regularly organizes conferences and meetings that are a breeding ground for the further development of skills and abilities. Take a look at the community pages for more information about the upcoming global conferences. Don't forget to browse Python's extensive documentation, email lists, and IRC channels as these are fanatical places to learn more about this powerful programming language and share your knowledge.

3. Powerful (and comprehensive) Standard Library

The strongest element of Python is the expanded Standard Library that allows you to program faster and more effectively on a wide variety of projects. This standard material can greatly simplify many complex coding tasks, making your codebase much more streamlined.

The Python Package Index (PyPII for short) has thousands of modules in its database. According to the last count, even more than 70,000. Some call this the "batteries included" philosophy of Python. Everything it takes to get started is included.

These packages help simplify and automate a wide variety of common tasks, including database access, desktop GUIs, scientific and numerical operations, education, networking, software and game development, and web application development. If you develop new modules that are specifically

Professor James A. Hendler of the University of Maryland has articulated his overriding reason for teaching Python to all of his undergraduate and master students who study computer science. He says, "Nothing has such great flexibility and as many web libraries as Python."

4. Scalable

Python is unique as a programming language that is ideal for use on both the smallest and largest scale. For those just starting an Informatics Training course and those working with Raspberry Pi, for example, to the largest use cases at research institutions and multinationals, Python are a perfect choice.

For users who need a powerful programming language, Python has proven itself as a leader for compute-intensive, critical applications for over a decade. For example, Disney, Lucasfilm, and Sony Dreamworks use Python coordinate clusters as powerful graphics workstations to render animations and other visuals for the most talked-about blockbuster movies.

Another great feature is IronPort, an email gateway system used by the largest ISPs and multinationals in the world. More than a million lines of encoding in Python allows this system to "keep it on the cutting edge," to say the words of Senior Director of Engineering Mark Peek.

Web applications suit Python very well. Several mature online frameworks enable rapid development and clean code for anyone developing a new interactive application. Of course, Python is also compatible with any WSGI-compliant web server. Add to that the fanatical support community, which has contributed greatly to Python's growing popularity, making it one of the most popular web development software languages for both large and small projects.

Python can handle even the largest web applications. The Python code behind YouTube, which organizes and offers millions of gigabytes of requested video all over the world, is a good example of this. "Python is fast enough for our site, it allows us to produce stable applications in record times with a minimum number of developers," said Cuong Do, a Software Architect at YouTube.

For an endless number of different user scenarios, Python provides a powerful, scalable, affordable, and easily expandable foundation for your programming project, where you can test and integrate prototypes and roll out systems quickly and efficiently. No wonder it's the most used, high-quality programming languages, the best choice for almost any software project.

Programming language

A programming language is a formal (or artificial, that is, a language with well-defined grammar rules) that gives a person, in this case, the programmer, the ability to write (or program) a series of instructions or sequences of orders in the form of algorithms in order to control the physical and/or logical behavior of a computer so that different kinds of data can be obtained or certain tasks can be performed. This whole set of commands written using a programming language is called a program.

Therefore, programming is the process of creating reliable software by writing, testing, debugging, compiling or interpreting, and maintaining the source code of said computer program. Basically, this process is defined by logically applying the following steps:

- The logical development of the program to solve a particular problem
- Writing the program logic using a specific programming language (program coding)
- Compilation or interpretation of the program until converting it into machine language
- Testing and debugging the program
- Documentation development.

Programming languages are made up of a set of symbols (called the alphabet), grammatical rules (lexical/morphological and syntactic), and semantics, which together define the valid structures of the language and its meaning. There is a common misconception that the terms 'programming language' and 'computer language' are synonyms. Encompass computer languages programming languages and others, such as HTML (language for marking of pages web that is not really a programming language, but a set of instructions that allow structuring the content of the documents).

The programming language allows you to specify precisely what data specific software should operate, how much data should be stored or transmitted, and what actions the software should take under a variety of circumstances. All this, through a language that tries to be relatively close to human or natural language. A relevant feature of programming languages is precise that more than one programmer can use a common set of instructions that are understood among them to carry out the construction of a program collaboratively.

History

In order for the computer to understand our instructions, a specific language known as machine code must be used, which the machine easily reads, but which is excessively complicated for people. In fact, it only consists of long strings of numbers 0 and 1.

To facilitate the work, the first computer operators decided to create a translator to replace 0s and 1s with words or abstraction of words; This is known as an assembly language. For example, to add the letter A of the English word add is added. Assembly language follows the same structure as machine language, but letters and words are easier to remember and understand than numbers.

The need to remember programming sequences for the usual actions led to naming them with easy to memorize and associate names: ADD(add), SUB(subtract), MUL(multiply), CALL(execute subroutine), etc. This sequence of positions was called "instructions," and this set of instructions was called assembly language. Later, different programming languages appeared, which receive their name because they have a syntactic structure similar to that of languages written by humans, also called high-level languages.

The first computer programmer expert was a woman: Ada Lovelace, daughter of Anabella Milbanke Byron and Lord Byron. Anabella introduced Ada to mathematics, which, after meeting Charles Babbage, translated and expanded the description of her analytical machine. Even though Babbage never finishes up the construction of any of her machines, Ada's work with them earned her the title of the world's first computer programmer. The name of the programming language Ada was chosen as a tribute to this programmer.

In late 1953, John Backus submitted a proposal to his superiors at IBM to develop a more practical alternative to the assembly language to program the mainframe IBM 704. The historic team Fortran of Backus consisted of programmers Richard Goldberg, Sheldon F. Best, Harlan Herrick, Peter Sheridan, Roy Nutt, Robert Nelson, Irving Ziller, Lois Haibt and David Sayre.

The first manual for language Fortran appeared in October 1956, with the first compiler Fortran delivered in April of 1957. This was an optimized compiler because customers were reluctant to use a high-level language unless their compiler could generate code whose performance was comparable to that of handmade assembly language code.

In 1960, COBOL, one of the languages still used today, was created in management computing.

As the complexity of the tasks computers performed increased, it became necessary to have a more efficient method of programming them. So high-level languages were created, as BASIC was in the versions introduced to microcomputers in the 1980s. While a task as simple as adding two numbers may require several instructions in assembly language, in a high-level language, a single statement will suffice.

Classification Of Programming Languages

Programming languages have historically been classified according to different criteria:

Historical classification

As new languages emerged that allowed for new, more expressive programming styles, these styles were distinguished over a series of generations, each representing programming languages that emerged in a similar era and with common generic characteristics.

High and low-level languages

Programming languages are usually classified into two broad categories that refer to their "level of abstraction," that is, as to how specific or general it is regarding the computing architecture inherent in the system being used.

Classification by paradigms

Programming paradigms distinguish different computational models and styles of structuring and organizing the tasks that a program must perform. A programming language can offer support to one or several programming paradigms, totally or partially.

Classification by purpose

Programming languages are the distinguished general purpose of that specific purpose.

Sometimes programming languages are also classified into families that share certain common characteristics such as the general style of the syntax they use. Usually, these characteristics are usually inherited from previous programming languages that served as inspiration for the creators of this language.

Historical or generational classification

Equipment computer (the hardware) has gone through four generations, of which the first three (computer valves, transistors, and integrated circuits) are very clear; the fourth (integrated circuits large scale) is more debatable.

Something similar has happened with the programming of computers (software), which is carried out in languages that are usually classified into five generations, of which the first three are evident, while not everyone agrees on the other two. These generations did not coincide exactly in time with those of hardware, but they did approximately, and are the following:

First-generation: the first computers were programmed directly in machine code (based on a binary system), which can be represented by sequences of 0 and 1. However, each computer model has its own internal structure when programming. These languages were called low-level language because their instructions exercise direct control over the hardware and are conditioned by the physical structure of the computers that support it. Since this type of language is much closer to machine logic than to human logic, it is much more complicated to program with it. The use of the word under in its denomination does not imply that the language is less powerful than a high-level language, but refers to the reduced abstraction between language and hardware. For example, these types of languages are used to schedule critical tasks for operating systems, real-time applications, or device drivers. Another limitation of these languages is that some programming knowledge is required to perform logical instruction sequences.

Second generation: symbolic languages, also typical of the machine, simplify the writing of instructions and make them more readable. This refers to the assembly language assembled through a macro assembler. It is the machine language combined with a series of powerful macros that allow you to declare complex data and control structures.

Third generation: high-level languages replace symbolic instructions with machine-independent codes, similar to human language or mathematics. They were created so that the common user could solve a data processing problem in an easier and faster way. They are used in computing environments where high performance is achieved with respect to languages of previous generations. Among them are C, FORTRAN, Smalltalk, Ada, C ++, C #, COBOL, Delphi, Java, and PHP, among others. Some of these languages may be general-purpose; that is, the language is not focused on a single specialty but can be used to create all kinds of programs. For certain more common tasks, there are libraries to facilitate programming that allows code reuse.

Fourth generation: this name has been given to certain tools that allow building simple applications by combining prefabricated parts. Today it is thought that these tools are not, properly speaking, and languages. It is worth mentioning that some propose to reserve the fourth generation name for object-oriented programming. The latter has a structure very similar to the other languages. Some of its features are: database access, graphic capabilities, automatic code generation, as well as being able to program visually (such as Visual Basic or SQL). Among its advantages are greater productivity and less exhaustion of the programmer, as well as less concentration on your part, since the tools provided include sequences of instructions. The level of concentration required is lower, since some instructions, which are given to the tools, in turn, include sequences of instructions at another level within the tool. When the previously developed programs have to be maintained, it is less complicated because it requires a lower level of concentration.

On the other hand, its disadvantages are that these pre-made tools are generally less flexible than direct instructions in low-level languages. In addition, dependencies are usually created with one or more external providers, which translate into a loss of autonomy. Likewise, often, these pre-made tools contain libraries from other providers, which entail installing additional options that are considered optional. Unless there are agreements with other providers, they are programs that run only in the language that created it. Nor do they usually meet international standards ISO and ANSI, which carries a future risk due to the fact that its time on the market is unknown. Some examples are NATURAL and PL / SQL.

Fifth-generation: Artificial intelligence languages are sometimes called that, although, with the failure of the fifth-generation Japanese project, this name has fallen into disuse.

Programming paradigm

A programming paradigm consists of a method for carrying out computations and the way in which the tasks that a program must perform must be structured and organized. It is a technological proposal adopted by a community of programmers, and developers whose central nucleus is unquestionable insofar as it only tries to solve one or several clearly defined problems; The resolution of these problems must consequently represent a significant advance in at least one parameter that affects software engineering. Represents a particular approach or philosophy to design solutions. The paradigms differ from each other in the concepts and the way of abstracting the elements involved in a problem, as well as in the steps that make up their solution to the problem, in other words, the computation. It has a close relationship with the formalization of certain languages at their defining moment. It is an employed programming style.

A programming paradigm is limited in time in terms of acceptance and uses because new paradigms provide new or better solutions that partially or totally replace it.

The programming paradigm that is currently most used is " object orientation " (OO). The central nucleus of this paradigm is the union of data and processing in an entity called "object," which in turn can be related to other "object" entities.

Traditionally, data and processing have been separated into different areas of software design and implementation. This caused large developments to have problems of reliability, maintenance, adaptation to changes, and scalability. With OO and features like encapsulation, polymorphism, or inheritance, significant advancement in software development was enabled at any production scale. The OO seems to be linked in its origins with languages like Lisp and Simula, although the first to coin the title of "object-oriented programming" was Smalltalk.

Classification by paradigms

In general, most paradigms are variants of the two main types of programming, imperative and declarative. In imperative programming, a set of instructions is described step by step that must be executed to vary the state of the program and find the solution, that is, an algorithm that describes the steps necessary to solve the problem.

In declarative programming, the sentences used are what they do is describe the problem you want to solve; It is programmed saying what you want to solve at the user level, but not the instructions necessary to solve it. The latter will be done through internal information inference mechanisms based on the description made.

Some of the different variants of programming paradigms are described below:

Imperative or procedural programming: It is the most widely used, it is based on giving instructions to the computer on how to do things in the form of algorithms, instead of describing the problem or solution. Cooking recipes and process checklists, despite not being computer programs, are also familiar concepts similar in style to imperative programming, where each step is an instruction. It is the most used and oldest form of programming; the main example is machine language. Examples of pure languages of this paradigm would be C, BASIC, or Pascal.

Object-oriented programming: It is imperative-based, but it encapsulates elements called objects that include both variables and functions. It is represented by C ++, C #, Java, or Python, among others, but the most representative would be the Smalltalk, which is completely object-oriented.

Dynamic programming: it is defined as the process of breaking problems into small parts in order to analyze and solve them as closely as possible to the optimum, it seeks to solve problems in O (n) without using recursive methods. This paradigm is more based on the way algorithms are performed, so it can be used with any imperative language.

Event-driven programming: this is a programming paradigm in which both the structure and the execution of programs are determined by the events that occur in the system, defined by the user or caused by them.

Declarative programming: it is based on describing the problem by stating properties and rules that must be followed, rather than instructions—their languages for functional programming, programming logic, or a logic-functional combination. The solution is obtained through internal control mechanisms, without specifying exactly how to find it (only the computer is told what it is that you want to obtain or what you are looking for). There are no destructive assignments, and the variables are used with referential transparency. Declarative languages have the advantage of being mathematically reasoned, which allows the use of mathematical mechanisms to optimize the performance of programs. Some of the earliest functional languages were Lisp and Prolog.

Functional programming: based on the definition of the predicates and is more mathematical, it is represented by Scheme (a variant of Lisp) or Haskell. Python also represents this paradigm.

Logical programming: based on the definition of logical relationships, it is represented by Prolog.

Programming with restrictions: similar to logic using equations. Almost all languages are variants of Prolog.

Multiparadigm programming: is the use of two or more paradigms within a program. The Lisp language is considered multi-paradigm. Like Python, it is object-oriented, thoughtful, imperative, and functional. As described by Bjarne Stroustrup, these languages allow you to create programs using more than one programming style. The goal in designing these languages is to allow programmers to use the best paradigm for each job, admitting that none solves all problems in the easiest and most efficient way possible. For example, programming languages like C ++, Genie, Delphi, Visual Basic, PHP, or D 6 combine the imperative paradigm with object-orientation. There are even multiparadigm languages that allow mixing in a natural way, as in the case of Oz, which has subsets (particularity of logical languages), and other characteristics typical of functional programming languages and object orientation. Another example is languages like Scheme of a functional paradigm or Prolog (logical paradigm), which have repetitive structures, typical of the imperative paradigm.

Reactive programming: this paradigm is based on the declaration of a series of objects emitting asynchronous events and another series of objects that "subscribe" to the former (that is, they listen to the emission of these events) and * they react * to the values they receive. It is very common to use Microsoft's Rx library (Acronym for Reactive Extensions), available for multiple programming languages.

Domain-specific language or DSL: this is the name of the languages developed to solve a specific problem, and can be entered into any previous group. The most representative would be declarative SQL for database management, but there are imperatives, such as the Logo.

Elements

Variables and vectors

The variables are titles assigned to memory spaces to store specific data. They are data containers, and therefore they differ according to the type of data they are capable of storing. In most programming languages, it is required to specify a specific type of variable to save specific data. For example, in Java, if we want to save a text string, we must specify that the variable is of type String. On the other hand, in languages like PHP or JavaScript This type of variable specification is not necessary. Also, there are compound variables called vectors. A vector is nothing more than a set of consecutive bytes in memory and of the same type stored within a container variable.

Conditionals

Conditional statements are code structures that indicate that for a certain part of the program to run, certain premises must be met; for example: that two values are the same, that one value exists, that one value is greater than another ... These conditions are generally only executed once throughout the program. The best known and used conditioning factors in programming are:

- If: Indicates a condition for a part of the program to be executed.

- Else if: It is always preceded by an "If" and indicates a condition for a part of the program to be executed as long as the condition of the previous if it does not meet and the one specified by the "else if" is met.
- Else: Always proceeded by "If" and sometimes by "Else If." It indicates that it should be run when the preconditions are not met.

Loops

Loops are close relatives of conditioners but constantly execute code as long as a certain condition is met. The most frequent are:

- For: Executes code while a variable is between 2 certain parameters.
- While: Executes code while the requested condition is met.

It must be said that although there are different types of loops, they are all capable of performing exactly the same functions. The use of one or the other depends, in general, on the taste of the programmer.

Features

The functions were created to avoid having to constantly repeat code snippets. A function could be considered as a variable that contains code within itself. Therefore, when we access this variable (the function), what we are actually doing is ordering the program to execute a certain predefined code above.

All programming languages have some primitive training elements for the description of the data and the processes or transformations applied to this data (such as the sum of two numbers or the selection of an element that is part of a collection). These primitive elements are defined by syntactic and semantic rules that describe their structure and meaning, respectively.

Syntax

The visible form of a programming language is known as syntax. Most programming languages are purely textual, that is, they use text sequences that include words, numbers, and punctuation, similar to natural written languages. Also, there are some programming languages that are more graphic in nature, using visual relationships between symbols to specify a program.

The syntax of a programming language describes the possible combinations of the symbols that form a syntactically accurate program. The meaning given to the combination of symbols is handled by their semantics (either formal or as part of the hard code of the implementation reference). Since most languages are textual, this article is about textual syntax.

The syntax of programming languages is generally defined using a combination of regular expressions (for the lexical/morphological structure) and the Backus-Naur notation (for the syntactic structure). This is an example of simple grammar, taken from the Lisp language:

expression :: = atom |

atom list :: = number | symbol

number :: = [+ -]? ['0' - '9'] +

symbol :: = ['A' - 'Z'] ['a' - 'z']. *

List :: = ' (' expression * ') '

With this grammar, the following is specified:

an expression can be an atom or a list ;

an atom can be a number or a symbol ;

a number is a continuous sequence of one or more decimal digits, optionally preceded by a plus sign or a minus sign;

a symbol is a letter that is followed by zero or more characters (excluding spaces); Y

a list is a pair of parentheses that open and close, with zero or more expressions in between.

Using natural language, for example, it may not be possible to assign meaning to a grammatically valid sentence or the sentence may be false:

- "Green and discolored ideas sleep furiously" is a grammatically well-formed sentence, but it has no commonly accepted meaning.
- "Juan is a married bachelor" is also grammatically well-formed but expresses a meaning that cannot be true.

Static semantics

Static semantics does define restrictions on the structure of valid texts that are impossible or very difficult to express using standard syntactic formalisms. For compiled languages, static semantics basically includes semantic rules that can be verified at compile time. For example, checking that each identifier is declared before being used (in languages that require such declarations) or that the labels in each arm of a case structure be different. Many important restrictions of this type, such as validating that identifiers are used in the appropriate contexts (for example, not adding an integer to the name of a function), or that subroutine calls have the appropriate number and type of parameters, can be implemented by defining them as rules in a logic known as a type system. Other forms of static analysis, such as data flow analysis, can also be part of static semantics. Other programming languages like Java and C # have defined assignment analysis, a form of data flow analysis, as part of their static semantics.

Type system

A data type system defines how a programming language classifies values and expressions into types, how those types can be manipulated, and how they interact. The purpose of a type system is to verify and usually enforce a certain level of accuracy in programs written in the language in question, detecting certain invalid operations. Any decidable type system has its advantages and disadvantages: while on the one hand, it rejects many incorrect programs, it also prohibits some correct but rare programs. In order to minimize this disadvantage, some languages include type gaps, explicit unverified conversions that can be used by the programmer to explicitly allow an operation not normally allowed between different types. In most typed languages, the type system is used only to verify the types of programs, but several languages, generally functional, carry out what is known as type inference, which takes the task away from the programmer. To specify the types. The formal design and study of the type systems are then known as type theory.

Typed languages versus non-typed languages

A language is said to be typed if the specification of each operation must define the data types for which it is applicable, with the implication that it is not applicable to other types. For example, "This Text in Quotation Marks" is a character string. In most programming languages, dividing the amount by a character string has no meaning. Therefore, most modern programming languages would reject any attempt to execute such an operation by any program. In some languages, these meaningless operations are detected when the program is compiled ("static" type validation) and are rejected by the compiler, while in others they are detected when the program is executed ("dynamic" type validation)

A special case of typed languages is single-type languages. These are often markup or scripting languages, such as REXX or SGML, and have only one data type, commonly character strings that are then used for both numeric and symbolic data.

In contrast, a language without types, as most assembly languages, allows any operation to be applied to any data, which generally are considered sequences of bits of various lengths. High-level languages without data include BCPL and some Forth varieties.

In practice, although few languages are considered to be typed from the point of view of type theory (that is, they verify or reject all operations), most modern languages offer some degree of type handling while many production languages provide means to bypass or bypass the typing system.

Static types versus dynamic types

In languages with static types, the type of all expressions is determined before the program is executed (typically when compiling).

Languages with static types can handle explicit types or inferred types. In the first case, the programmer must write the types in certain textual positions. In the second case, the compiler does infer the types of the expressions and the declarations according to the context. Most popular languages with static types, such as C ++, C #, and Java, handle explicit types. Total inference of types is usually associated with less popular languages, such as Haskell and ML. However, many explicit type languages allow partial type inferences; both Java and C #, for example, infer types in a limited number of cases.

Languages with dynamic types determine the validity of the types involved in operations during the execution of the program. In other words, types are associated with running values instead of textual expressions. As in the case of inferred type languages, languages with dynamic types do not require the programmer to write the types of expressions. Among other things, this allows the same variable to be associated with values of different types at different times during the execution of a program. However, type errors cannot be detected automatically until the code is executed, making it difficult to debug programs, however, in languages with dynamic types, debugging is usually left out in favor of development techniques such as BDD and TDD. Ruby, Lisp, JavaScript, and Python are languages with dynamic types.

Weak and strong types

Languages weakly typed allow a value of a type can be treated as another type; for example, a chain can be operated as a number.

This can be useful at times, but it can also allow certain types of flaws that cannot be detected during compilation or sometimes not even during execution.

Languages strongly typed prevent pass above. Any attempt to perform an operation on the wrong type triggers an error. Languages with strong types are often called safe types.

Languages with weak fonts like Perl and JavaScript allow a large number of implicit type conversions. For example, in JavaScript expression, 2 * x implicitly converted x to a number, and this conversion is successful even when x it is null, undefined a Array or a string of letters. These implicit conversions are often useful, but they can also hide programming errors.

The characteristics of static and strong are now generally considered orthogonal concepts, but their treatment in different texts varies. Some use the term strong types to refer to strongly static types or to increase confusion, simply as the equivalence of static types. So C has been called both strong type language and weak static type language.

Implementation

A language implementation is one that provides a way for a program to run for a certain combination of software and hardware. There are basically two ways to implement a language: compilation and interpretation.

Compilation: is the process that translates a program written in one programming language into another programming language, generating an equivalent program that the machine will be able to interpret. The translator programs that can perform this operation are called compilers. These, like advanced assembly programs, can generate many lines of machine code for each proposition in the source program.

Interpretation: it is an assignment of meanings to the well-formed formulas of a formal language. Since formal languages can be defined in purely syntactic terms, their well-formed formulas may be no more than strings of symbols without any meaning. An interpretation gives meaning to those formulas.

An alternative can also be used to translate high-level languages. Instead of translating the source program and permanently burning the object code produced during compilation for use in a future run, the programmer only loads the source program onto the computer along with the data to be processed. Next, an interpreter program, stored in the operating system on the disk, or permanently embedded within the machine, converts each proposition of the source program into machine language as needed during data processing. The object code is not saved for later use.

The next time an instruction is used; it must be interpreted again and translated into machine language. For example, during repetitive processing of the steps in a loop or cycle, each instruction in the loop will have to be reinterpreted with each repeated execution of the loop, which makes the program slower at runtime (because it goes reviewing the code at runtime) but faster at design time (because you don't have to compile the entire code at all times). The interpreter eliminates the need to compile after each modification of the program when you want to add functions or correct errors;

Most high-level languages allow multipurpose programming, although many of them were designed to allow dedicated programming, as was Pascal with mathematics at its beginning.

Children's educational languages , such as Logo, have also been implemented through a series of simple instructions. Currently, some languages specially indicated for web applications are very popular, such as Perl, PHP, Ruby, Python, or JavaScript.

Technique

When writing programs that provide the best results, a number of details should be considered.

- Correction. A program is correct if it does what it should do as established in the phases prior to its development. To determine if a program does what it should, it is very important to clearly specify what the program should do before developing it and, when finished, compare it with what it actually does.

- Clarity. It is very important that the program is as clear and readable as possible to facilitate its development and subsequent maintenance. When developing a program, you should try to make its structure simple and coherent, as well as taking care of the style in the edition; In this way, the programmer's work is facilitated, both in the creation phase and in the subsequent phases of error correction, extensions, modifications, etc. Phases can be performed even by another programmer, making clarity even more necessary so that other programmers can continue the work easily. Some programmers even use ASCII Artto delimit sections of code. Others, for fun or to prevent a comfortable analysis to other programmers, resort to the use of obfuscated code.

- Efficiency. It is that the program, in addition to doing what it was created for (that is, being correct), does so by managing the resources it uses in the best possible way. Normally, when talking about the efficiency of a program, it usually refers to the time it takes to perform the task for which it was created and the amount of memory it needs, but there are other resources that can also be considered when obtaining efficiency of a program, depending on its nature (disk space it uses, network traffic it generates, etc.).

- Portability. A program is portable when it has the ability to run on a platform, whether hardware or software, different from the one on which it was developed. Portability is a highly desirable feature for a program, since it allows, for example, a program that has been developed for GNU / Linux systems to run in the Windows family of operating systems as well. This allows the program to reach more users more easily.

Paradigms

Programs can be classified by the language paradigm used to produce them. The main paradigms are imperatives, declarative, and object orientation.

Programs that use an imperative language specify an algorithm, use declarations, expressions, and statements. A statement associates a variable name with a data type, for example, var x: integer; an expression contains a value, for example, 2 + 2contains the value 4. Finally, a judgment must assign an expression to a variable or use the value of a variable to alter the flow of a program, for example, x:= 2 + 2; if x == 4, then haz_algo();. A common criticism is imperative languages are the effect of assignment statements on a class of variables called "nonlocal."

Programs that use declarative language specify the properties that the output should know about and do not specify any implementation details. Two broad aspects of declarative languages are functional languages and logical languages. Functional languages do not allow assignments of non-local variables; thus, programs such as mathematical functions are made easier, for example. The principle behind logical languages is to define the problem to be solved (the objective) and leaves the details of the solution to the system. The objective is defined by giving a list of sub-objectives. Each sub-objective is also defined by giving a list of its sub-objectives, etc. If in trying to find a solution, a sub-target route fails, then such a sub-target is dropped, and another route is systematically tested.

The way in which it is programmed can be through text or visually. In visual programming, the elements are manipulated graphically instead of being specified by means of text.

How to Be a Software Developer?

Para many people to be software developer may seem magical or work for nerds who still live with their mothers, however, is not as complex or as alien to the reality of mortals simple as it might seem.

For starters, I want to say to those new entrepreneurs who dream of being tech greats like Elon Musk or Mark Zuckerberg, that it is not as simple as the TV series or the media would lead you to believe, but not so complex as to be impossible!

Discipline is the key to everything, even if it sounds cliche!

A few years ago, you might think that the only way to build software programs or work for software factories was to prepare to be an engineer, learn a lot of math, physics, theories, paradigms, and programming patterns and finally start coding like crazy.

What matters is your desire and your ability to learn and transform.

How can I affirm this?

In the past, being a software developer could be more complex, the environment was not as evolved as now, and when they told you about programs, you thought of developments that took rockets to the moon, standardized military communications or managed wall street, however, today Nowadays you can make software of any type and for the simplest things, therefore, getting started is much easier.

There are countless online courses, books, meetups, boot camps, and YouTube videos, among other resources, that provide a giant gateway to the world of technology without having to go through a university.

Although some projects require knowledge of linear programming, integer programming, optimization, heuristics, integral differential equations, and other things from nerds.

From my perspective, a large number of startups or emerging technology companies have come to expand the paradigm of what was previously considered a "suitable person" to be a developer. Although knowledge is still important, being is gaining importance over knowledge; that is, your ability to learn and transform yourself and who you are as a person are bearing the same weight as your experience and knowledge when applying for a job.

There are projects of all kinds, from software that allows you to perform high-risk operations using robotic arms remotely, where you may have to have a solid academic background, to applications in which burritos are sold, where perhaps what matters Be your creativity on how to transform said ecosystem.

The requirements to start learning are minimal, a pc, internet, and your desire.

I could mention many more reasons why I think anyone can start a career in the world of technology; however, I want to conclude with the most important one.

If day by day you work for what you want, you read, you learn, and you progress you can achieve your goals, I say it from my own experience, I am not a software engineer certified by a university,

I am an electronic engineer who taught himself to make software at a professional level.

This is why I invite anyone who wants to be part of the tech world from their heart, regardless of their academic or professional level, to start learning and climbing until we say, who knows, they can be the Elon Musks of Latin America.

How to start

The acquisition of knowledge and the ability to apply it is the basis of everything. Choose a topic in which you would like to start such as mobile application development (Android, Ios), web development (Javascript, HTML, CSS3, Angular, React, Node ... to infinity and beyond ...), desktop application development (JAVA, C ++, C #) or any type of software development that catches your attention.

Find out about state of the art.

Look for information on what it is to develop the technology you want to develop, news, forums, official pages, in short, any information that, although not very relevant, gives you a context of what it is to develop such technology, what it is for and its principles.

Start with the most basic.

Having chosen your startup technology and generated a context, start with the most basic language. Delve into the programming language or languages that are part of the core (the fundamental set of technologies) of the type of development you chose.

For example, for web development, you could start by learning how to make web applications that run in the browser. These applications at their purest basis are made with HTML5, CSS3 (markup languages), and Javascript (programming language). In this way, starting by reading and learning about each of these three languages would be essential, and you could do the same with any of the other types of software development.

Go ahead with your first program or follow some start guide that allows you to make your first development effort in a simple way, and that leads you to take ownership of the bases. Here are some examples of "Getting started" or startup guides.

- Android
- Express server
- HTML

Delve into the methodology.

When you feel that you have more ownership of your study topic, start to inquire about what patterns, forms of development, development frameworks, libraries, and other things that bring you closer to being a professional in software development.

Practice makes a master.

Continue building software; in the end, the best way to learn is by practicing and practicing, with each new project includes new objectives more difficult than the previous ones. If you do not know what to do or where to start, use some web search engine (Google, yahoo), and I assure you that you will find many pages that are dedicated to teaching through the creation of projects: codigofacilto, udemy, Platzi and thousands more. Similarly, there are many free resources as paid resources; it is only a matter of knowing how to search.

Reach level 100.

As in video games, everything consists of going level by level, go step by step, and do not rush; at some point, you will find yourself right where you want to be, and it may be sooner than you expect. When you feel that you are prepared to face new challenges and that you have a solid knowledge of your development area, create software that is useful, you could even publish it, and it may or may not be sold, the important thing is to consolidate all the knowledge you have acquired and have material for teaching your future clients or companies that want to hire you.

Get closer to the professional environment.

Tell the world that you are ready to solve their problems. Be honest with yourself, and when you find that your knowledge is sufficient to solve the problems of others, start looking for internships in software companies or jobs that do not require extensive experience. Socializing and building software as a team is one of the best ways to grow as a developer.

Evaluate yourself and continue.

Finally, in your personal construction process, you will find that you have the capabilities to continue advancing, start an enterprise, look for a job as a developer or follow the path you want because, at this moment, you will be one more colleague. Do not forget to continue learning day by day and not keep a single technology; over time, your level and professional experience will demonstrate who you are.

You may encounter many obstacles but continue!

It is possible that on the way you want to go you will encounter obstacles, people who do not believe in you, companies that belittle you, "Ah, aren't you a software engineer?" or even yourself you set limits, however, what you create and build will be what will speak for you.

What Is CSS For?

CSS is a language used to give presentation and appearance of "style" to web pages (HTML documents). CSS is not a programming language. We could say that it is a language that usually appears related or close to a programming language or that it usually collaborates with a programming language, but it is not a programming language per se.

Sometimes you will hear of "HTML and CSS programming languages." This expression is, from the formal point of view, incorrect, since neither HTML nor CSS is programming languages. However, sometimes the term "CSS programming" is used colloquially.

A programming language is a language that is used to carry out processes of interest through a computer or electronic device, from a calculation for a student or engineer, to an online purchase, through anything you can think of. A programming language has as basic characteristics having the ability to "make decisions" or execute one process or another depending on the circumstances (for example, depending on the button that the user presses), as well as being able to repeat processes repeatedly until a condition is met. CSS is not a language that allows fulfilling these functions; therefore, it is not a programming language even though it is used together with programming languages.

CSS is a language that appeared to make web development easier and better looking. Web development comprises multiple areas of knowledge:

In the classification that we have made, CSS would be included within the area of graphic design and layout.

Web developments have very variable dimensions. We can talk from a small website for a local company to a large portal for an international company. In both cases, we could say that web programming and web design intervene. However, a small development can be carried out by a single person that encompasses both programming and design, while a large development requires a more or less extensive work team and with different specialists, since around web developments there are different areas of knowledge involved (analysis, design, programming, systems, integration, testing, etc.).

In a large development, there are people specialized in different areas, so the programmer does not usually work on the design (except to make some adjustments or changes, or to solve problems). However, it is convenient for a web programmer to have the basic knowledge of CSS since it will be useful and necessary, on the one hand, for solving problems and, on the other hand, to integrate issues where design and programming intermingle.

If we look at the languages or technologies that exist around web developments, we could make a classification that includes: HTML, CSS, Databases, Servers, Client-side programming languages (e.g., Javascript), and Programming languages on the server-side (e.g., PHP).

HTML and CSS are technologies (or metalanguages, since they cannot be considered programming languages) that intervene in practically every development, large or small. They are in charge of providing a pleasant structure and presentation to what the user of web pages sees.

The server-side programming languages perform processes on the server (the remote computer that is responsible for sending web pages over the internet): we can cite among these Java (JSP), ASP.NET, PHP, or Perl languages, between main.

The client-side programming languages carry out processes on the user's personal computer (visual effects, calculations, etc.): we can cite among these languages Javascript, Java (applets), or VBScript, among the main ones.

Regarding databases, we can name MySQL, SQLServer, and Oracle, among the main ones.

Technologies combine with each other in many different ways. We can mention some quite common combinations between programming languages and databases: Java + Oracle, ASP.NET + SQLServer, PHP + MySQL. Whichever combination is used, in modern web development, HTML and CSS will always intervene.

In summary, CSS is a language to give presentation and style to web pages whose basic aspects must be known by web developers as well as web designers or web designers. In practice, many times, the programming code is intermixed with the HTML code and CSS code, which is why we talk colloquially about "web programming" to refer to this whole set, although formally neither HTML nor CSS are programming languages.

Note that we are trying to make clear what CSS is and what it is for before starting to study this language because if we have clear concepts, it will be much easier for us to learn, we will save time and make fewer mistakes.

Java, The Programming Language That Will Open The Doors To Your Next Job

This information is important if you are actively searching for a job. Whether you are a web programmer and want to turn your professional career around, or you want to start in this world of source code development, training in Java technology may be the key to your future.

Another index that also yields very encouraging data for Java programmers is the Pluralsight Technology Index (PTI), which classifies software development technologies according to their popularity, taking as reference 8 billion data collected from the internet. This year Java leads this ranking, being another important indication of the future importance of this programmatic language.

Currently, many companies are seeking applicants to have skills in handling Java for web development. This detail makes these profiles different from the rest, although they incorporate knowledge in other types of languages such as Phyton, C or C ++, they do not include Java.

You may wonder why that job advantage if they also control web development. Easy. The vast majority of companies have decided to carry out all their software and application programming projects in the Java language. This is due to its great versatility and the possibility of developing multiplatform projects.

Another feature that has made it the most popular language is the security it offers, a very precious aspect given that cyber-attacks are becoming more frequent every time. If it is important for many, it is vital for others as it is in the banking and financial industry.

Java has risen from the ashes

In recent years, many programming languages have been launched on the market, leading Java to a complicated situation since it was becoming obsolete. But, thanks to the rapid reaction of the company and incorporating new functionalities that until now did not exist, they have turned Java into a very strong rival.

Java has undoubtedly managed to take advantage of bad times, and adapt to changes, regaining its popularity.

A safe bet

Not only the fact of being a very popular language is what makes Java the best option, but also the facilities it offers when it comes to learning the code. Java should be the base language for any self-respecting programmer; from this base, you can learn the rest in a very simple way.

You want to develop your opportunities to find a job, sign up for our video course "Fundamentals of programming in Java. Bases of computing". The future is in Java.

Functional programming

Functional programming is a declarative programming paradigm, whereby we manage our code in a different way, based on the use and behavior of mathematical functions and which has been explicitly created to allow a purely functional approach to problem-solving.

Perhaps the above does not tell you much, and that is that functional programming is one of those things that are very difficult to explain to people without a programming background or in mathematics. However, let's say that it goes beyond how we structure and organize our code; in functional programming, other concepts such as pure functions, referential integrity, and the use of higher-order functions come into consideration.

About declarative programming and imperative, I don't want them to get overwhelmed. Basically, because it is an advanced topic that we will talk about in another article and also because most modern languages are flexible enough to support various paradigms.

For example, Swift is therefore compatible with the imperative programming paradigm as the paradigm of declarative programming, just as C #, the latter includes extensions of the language that explicitly were designed to be compatible with the functional and declarative programming, including expressions lambda, type inference and I to technology LINQ.

Functional programming is a very broad topic to which we will dedicate a full article, so I take this opportunity to invite you to follow us on our social networks and subscribe to our mailing list so that you do not miss any of our future publications.

Before continuing, let's name some of the advantages that functional programming offers compared to the imperative:

- Testing functional code is easier since we do not depend on a state that can be altered from anywhere. Our output for the same input will always be the same.
- Concurrent or parallel programming is also much simpler. Since we do not depend on variables to be synchronized, nor do we have to implement methods in order to validate that only certain blocks can be accessed through a single thread, something that greatly helps us to make everything much simpler.
- Applications are written with functional code typically have far fewer lines of code. Aside from the characteristics of each of the languages, by being able to pass and return functions as parameters, our code is much more reusable and easier to maintain.
- There are also certain drawbacks with functional programming or let's say perhaps, nuances that sometimes may not be entirely ideal, but we will see these in the section we will dedicate to the subject.

The most popular programming languages

In the definition of the programming language, we talked about how machines and programmers could understand each other to obtain the expected result. Well, there is an international general index, the TIOBE Index, which tells us which are the most used or popular. So far this year, TIOBE has pointed out the Java, C, C ++, Python, C # and Javascript languages.

This index is elaborated thanks to variables such as the number of qualified programmers, the labor demand, the interest in the community after searches on engines such as Google and Bing, or the demand for courses for one language or another.

Programming software

Programming software or rather the software that we use to develop applications is nothing more than a set of all those tools that allow us to write code, aimed at creating, debugging, maintaining and packaging our projects.

These development suites are usually made up of small programs that manage some of the different stages that our project will go through during its creation. Some of them are:

- Code editors: Through these, we write our code and obtain auto-complete services, marking of syntactic errors, as well as refactoring.
- Compilers: We have talked about them before, and they translate the source code into machine language. They generate executable binaries; these are usually where the direct link icons you have on your desktop point to.
- Debuggers. They are a great ally of programmers; they serve us to monitor the execution of a program line by line, keeping track of the values of certain variables, references to objects in memory, helping us to correct those errors that are not obvious and therefore optimizing our development time.

IDE (Integrated Development Environment)

The IDE (Integrated Development Environment) or Integrated Development Environment, is nothing more than that programming software.

As we already know, an IDE is a computer application that programmers use, and that provides a series of services that facilitate software programming.

Currently, we have some very complete and complex, but generally, they have a graphical interface in which all their options are concentrated at our disposal: a source code editor, self-complete services, integration with version control systems, database connection management, device simulators:

.. A debugger to streamline the software development process, among many other features.

Visual Studio

Microsoft Visual Studio in a fairly famous IDE, with support for multiple programming languages and which is usually associated with the development of applications on Microsoft Windows platforms and this, is correct, but we have to point out the steps it has taken towards Open Source, In fact, we already have relatively complete versions for macOS and Linux.

Visual Studio enables developers to create web sites and applications, as well as web services in any environment with support for the .NET platform. Thus, applications can be created that communicate between workstations, web pages, mobile devices, embedded devices, and video game consoles, among others.

Xcode

Xcode is an IDE of the most advanced in the market. It has everything you may need during the development of applications for Apple platforms. Xcode is incredibly fast and stable as you work, even editing the largest files. It has powerful new refactoring features, renaming symbols through Swift, and even user interface files.

This format provides design and development engineering for the creation of applications (always talking about iPhone, Mac, and iPad, at least for the moment) that you cannot miss, especially if you intend to dedicate yourself to programming.

Code Editors

Code editors emerged as a lighter alternative to classic IDEs, and with a clear focus on productivity. Initially, they were widely used in web development, but currently, they have support for almost all programming languages. Let's see the most representative:

Visual Studio Code

As you can imagine, this code editor is developed by Microsoft, it is free, multiplatform, and currently one of the most used worldwide, even on Linux and macOS systems where historically there has been some reluctance to use Microsoft products.

Atom

Atom is developed by GitHub, it is a free source code editor, and through which we can manage our software projects, it is also cross-platform and open source. It has very good documentation, it is a very flexible editor that we can customize to taste, it has support for plug-ins written in Node.js, and the integration of Git is great... it is made by GitHub after all!

If there is a downside to Atom, it is that it sometimes feels slow. There are times when we open a large file or switch between tabs if we have many open, it is where we notice a delay, there is a certain delay that is quite annoying and even more so when we have powerful computers where this should never happen.

The performance problem is not new, since its inception, this was already talked about, it was a topic quite debated by the entire community, but many wanted to give it a try, it was a project of the guys from GitHub (of which we are all fans), it was new, and it was in beta phase, it will improve! We said many. Certainly, it was, it has taken a qualitative leap since then, but the frustration is still there, less frequently, but it still persists.

An atom is a great tool, especially for those who want to customize their editor easily, and beyond what others offer. As a developer, the freedom to modify, add, and expand your editor gives you an incredible feeling of power. I also love your documents. The Atom Flight Manual provides an excellent starting point for new users.

Atom was very popular and, in part, still is, but currently, many developers have advocated other alternatives and are actively using Visual Studio Code.

Everything we have seen in this article should already give us an idea of those languages that make many of the applications we use every day work, and although they may be developed with different programming languages, almost all of them have common bases that make learning any of these are relatively easy tasks once you have mastered them.

Now you may be asked what a programming language is? You undoubtedly have the basic knowledge to be able to establish a conversation and even a debate on this. We hope we have solved all your doubts or some of them, and in the best of cases, we have guided you when choosing your next educational or work goal.

Conclusion

One of the big problems they face when starting in this programming world is that when you start you want to make complex programs, pages, and professional applications, but at the critical moment there can be some difficulties, even when you have the experience, for this reason, we decided to share some tips to shorten the learning curve:

1-Know the origins first.

This does not mean that you completely learn the history of the computer, but you must know it, that will give you the notion of how everything came about, so you will know how everything works, from data to an operating system.

2-Master basic concepts.

Know computer concepts such as what is a data, record, field, information among others. As theoretical and boring as this may seem, it will help a future to understand how multiple functions work and why they are made that way.

3- Make an algorithm before starting to throw codes.

If you do not know what it is sincerely I tell you that you will less understand what you do, this is a serious mistake that many programmers make that we do not give importance to the analysis before starting, I advise you that if you are starting as a programmer, you first practice informal algorithms, then it happens to the computations.

This will open up your logic as a programmer and will make a kind of connection between your mind and the computer so that both friends can easily understand.

4-Study fundamental functions of programming

When we start as a programmer, it is necessary that we know perfectly the functions like for "for," while "while," if "if" but "else," among others, where our code starts, because it must have an end and a set of fundamental operations that are in general use.

And you will ask yourself: What is all this for me to learn any programming language? Simple and straightforward programming in general, and in any programming language be it Python, PHP, C ++, C, C #, Java, etc. a "for" will remain a "for" an "if" will continue to be "if" and a "function" will continue to be "function" the only thing that varies are the details of the language's own syntax.

5-Anyone can program

You must trust yourself and be persevering, what makes good programmers is not that they have exceptional talent better than everyone or anything like that, rather they know and master the concepts that I have mentioned before, This means that they are made to learn both a new language and to understand well what they do as programmers.

Be patient read, study, use the documentation that is offered, one of my teachers says that when he started as a programmer he made many mistakes, and it was very difficult to adapt to programming, today he is one of the best and most recognized programmers from my country.

If you take these tips to the letter, success as a programmer awaits you, and many doors will open in this wonderful world of technology.

Made in the USA
Monee, IL
18 December 2021

86324284R00058